JESUS CHRIST
Your King

C. W. Tullis

Gotham Books

30 N Gould St.
 Ste. 20820, Sheridan, WY 82801
https://gothambooksinc.com/

Phone: 1 (307) 464-7800

© 2026 *C.W. Tullis*. All rights reserved.

No part of this book may be reproduced, stored in a retrieval system, or transmitted by any means without the written permission of the author.

Published by Gotham Books (February 17, 2026)

ISBN: 979-8-3302-9632-3 (H)
ISBN: 979-8-3302-9630-9 (P)
ISBN: 979-8-3302-9631-6 (E)

Because of the dynamic nature of the Internet, any web addresses or links contained in this book may have changed since publication and may no longer be valid.

The views expressed in this work are solely those of the author and do not necessarily reflect the views of the publisher, and the publisher hereby disclaims any responsibility for them.

CONTENTS

Introduction

Verse 1

Verse 2

Verse 3

Refrain

Ending

Music

References

Acknowledgement

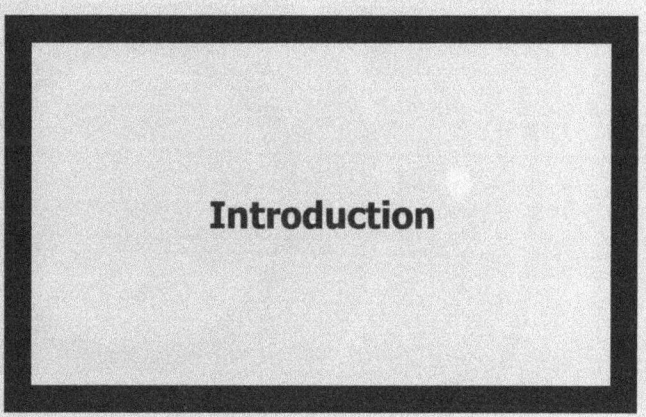

Introduction

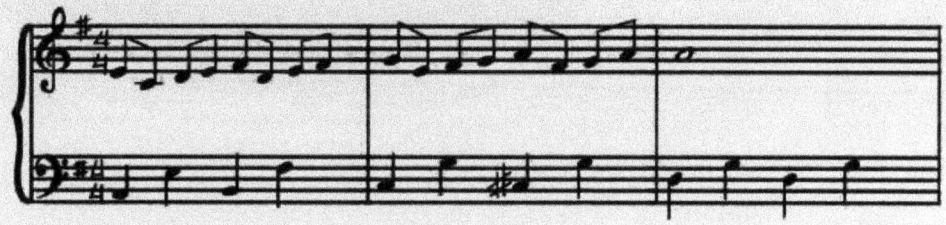

that He gave His only

begotten son.

Verse 1:

A luminary light,

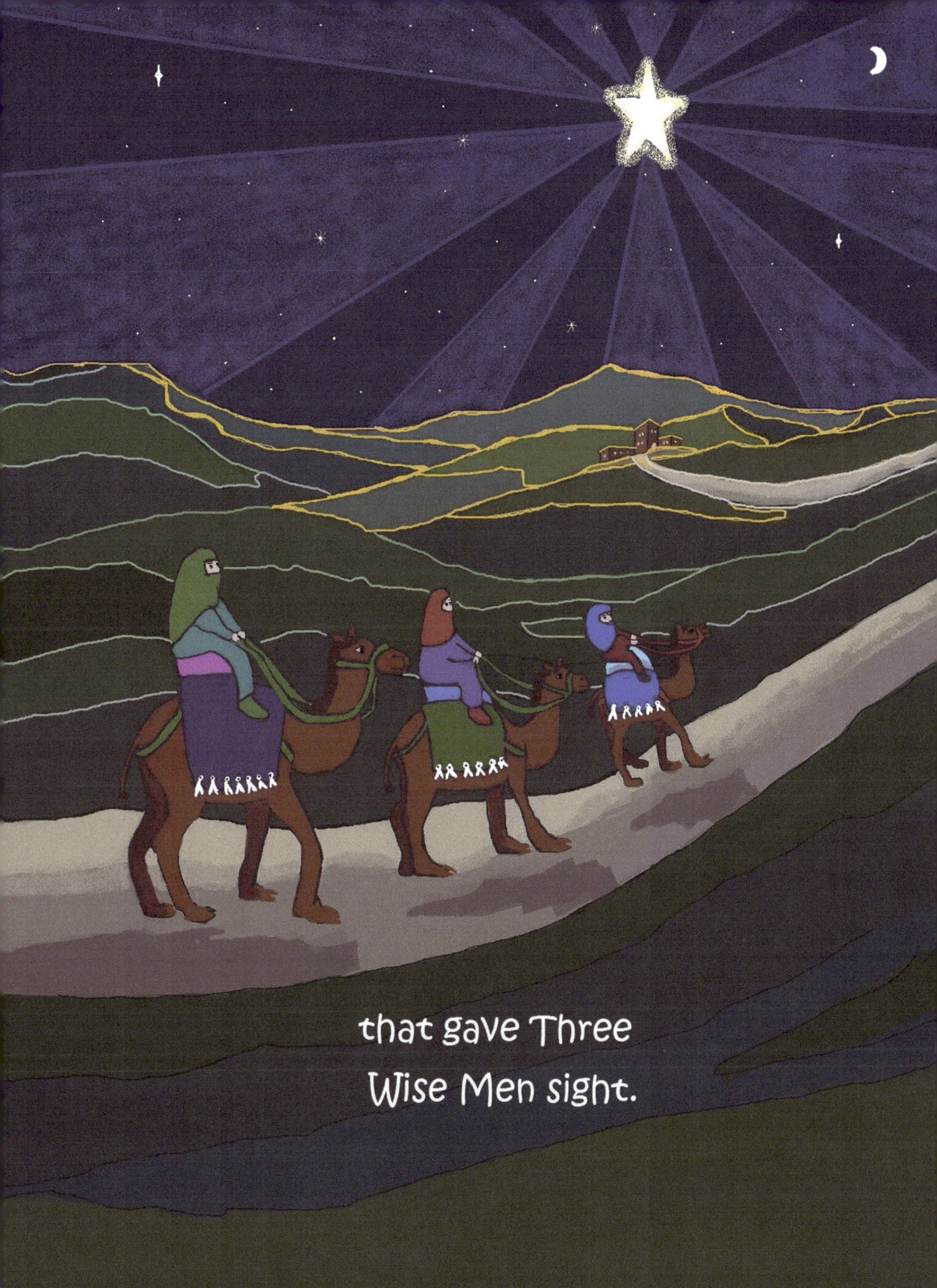

that God gave to the earth.

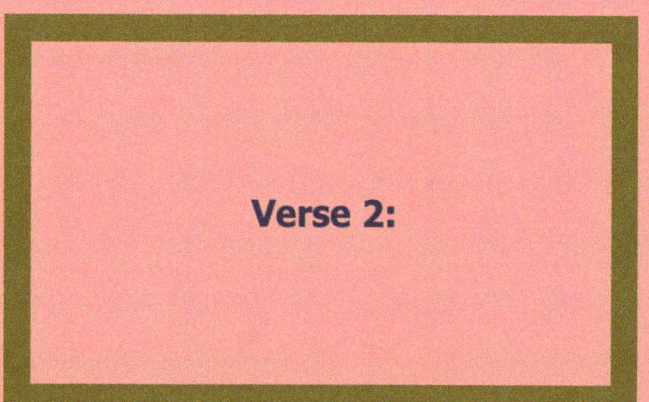

Verse 2:

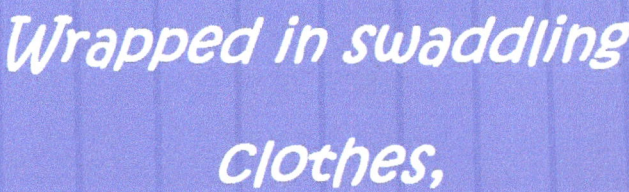
Wrapped in swaddling clothes,

He was born to save,

God's newborn babe.

Verse 3:

When an angel appeared

For I bring to all of you,

and all will sing and say.

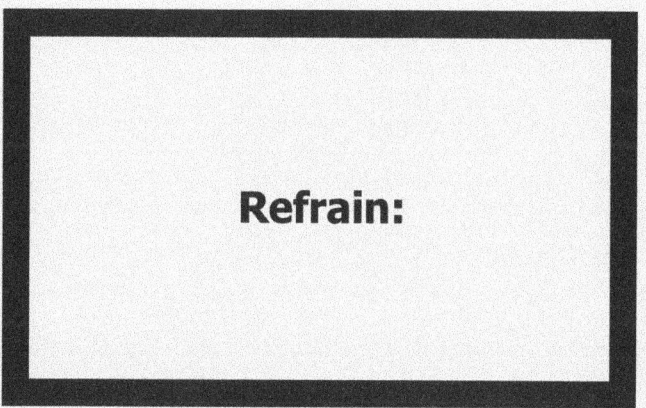

and thank Him over and over.

His pure white fleece,

the Prince of Peace,

Ending:

MUSIC

With Chords

Medium Scale:

B7 = D# F# A B   D = D F# A   Em = E G B

G = D G B   G+ = D# G B   Dsus4 = D G A

Am = C E A   A = C# E A   Bm = D F# B

G7 = D F G B   C = C E G

Lower Scale:

G = B D G   D = A D F#

JESUS CHRIST YOUR KING

References:

REFERENCES:

To introduction

Holman Home Bible: King James Version, Pg. 1089, John 3:16,
"For God so loved the world, that He gave His only begotten son, that
Whosoever believeth in him should not perish, but have everlasting life."

<u>Hark</u>: the Random House Dictionary of the English language, College Edition 1968, Pg. 603, 2: "To listen, to hear"

<u>Herald</u>: The Random House Dictionary of the English Language, College Edition 1968, Pg 618, 4: "a person or thing that proclaims or announces"

There is another song that has <u>Hark! The Herald Angels Sing</u>: written by music: Felix Mendelssohn; arranged by William H. Cummings and text: by Charles Wesley,

<u>Glory</u>: Is another word for Praise. From the Random House Dictionary of the English Language, College edition, 1968, Pg, 561 "exalted <u>praise</u>, honor"

Holman Home Bible: King James Version, pg. 1048, St. Luke2:14, Glory to God in the highest, and on the earth peace, good will toward men.

<u>God so loved the world, that He gave His only begotten Son</u>
<u>"Hark the herald, the angel's sings, alleluia, Praise the King"</u>

Verse 1.

Holman Home Bible: King James Version, Pg. 984, St. Matthew2:2, "Saying, where is he that is born King of the Jews? For we have seen his <u>star</u> in the east, and are come to worship him".

Holman Home Bible: King James Version, Pg. 984, St. Matthew 2:9 "When they heard the king, they departed; and, low, the <u>star</u>, which they saw in the east, went before them, till it came and stood over where the young child was".

Holmon Home Bible, King James Version, Pg. 984. St. Matthew 2:10 "When they saw the <u>star</u>, they rejoiced with exceeding great joy."

Luminary: The Random House Dictionary of the English Language, College Edition, 1968, Pg. 797, 1. "A celestial body, as the sun of moon". 2. "a body, object, etc., that gives light"

Magi: The Random House Dictionary of the English Language, College Edition, 1968, Pg. 804, "the three wise men who paid homage to the infant Jesus"

Holman Home Bible, King James Version, Pg, 983, 984. St. Matthew: 2:1 "Now When Jesus was born in Bethlehem of Judea in the days of Herod the king behold, there came wise men from the east to Jerusalem".

On this blessed night, was a star that shone so bright

A luminary light, that gave three wise men sight

They traveled so far, in search of His star

To see this child's birth, that God gave to the earth.

Verse 2.

Meek: The Random House Dictionary of the English Language, College Edition, 1968, Pg. 831, 3. "Obs. Gentle; kind;"

Mild: The Random House Dictionary of the English Language, College Edition, 1968, Pg. 847, 1." Gentle or temperate in feeling or behavior towards others."

Manger: The Random House Dictionary of the English Language, College Edition 1968, pg. 813, 1. " a box or trough from which horses or cattle eat". Holman Home Bible, King James Version, Pg. 1048, St. Luke 2:7 "and she brought forth her firstborn son, and wrapped him in swaddling clothes and laid him in a manger; because there was no room for them in the inn".

Holman Home Bible, King James Version, Pg. 1048, St. Luke 2:12 "And this shall be a sign unto you; Ye shall find the babe wrapped in swaddling clothes, Laying in a manger".

Holman Home Bible, King James Version, Pg. 1048, St. Luke 2:16 "And they came in haste, and found Mary and Joseph, and the babe lying in a <u>manger</u>".

<u>Swaddling clothes</u>: *The Random House Dictionary of the English Language, College Edition, 1968, Pg 1325, 1. "clothes consisting of long narrow strips of cloth for swaddling an infant".*

<u>Swaddling</u>: *The Random House Dictionary of the English Language, College Edition, 1968, Pg, 1325, 1. "to bind (an infant, esp. a newborn infant) with long narrow strips of cloth to prevent free movement."*

Holman Home Bible, King James Version, Pg. 1089, St. John 3:17 "For God sent not his Son into the world to condemn the world; but that the world through him might be <u>saved</u>".

<u>*He was meek and mild, this sweet little child*</u>

<u>*In a manger He lay, on a fresh bed of hay*</u>

<u>*Wrapped in swaddling clothes, from head to toes*</u>

<u>*He was born to save, God's new born babe.*</u>

Verse 3.

<u>Shepherd</u>: *The Random House Dictionary of the English language, College Edition, 1968, Pg. 1212, 1213, 1. "man who herds, tends, and guards sheep".*

Holman Home Bible, King James Version, Pg. 1048, St. Luke 2:10 "And the angel said unto them, fear not: for, behold, I bring you good tidings of great joy, which shall be to all people."

<u>Tidings</u>: *The Random House Dictionary of the English Language, College Edition 1968, Pg. 1373, "(sometimes construed as sing.) <u>news</u>, information, or report;".*

<u>*Shepherd's watched over their sheep, while some were a sleep*</u>

When and Angel appeared, and said don't fear

For I bring to all of you, great joyous news

Your King was born today, and all will sing and say

Refrain:

<u>Praise</u>: The Random House Dictionary of the English Language, College Edition 1968, Pg. 1041, 2. "The offering of grateful homage in words or song, as an act of worship".

<u>Jehovah</u>: The Random House Dictionary of the English Language, College Edition 1968, Pg. 717, 1. "a name of God in the old Testament, an erroneous rendering of the ineffable name, JHVH, in the Hebrew Scriptures".

<u>Jehovah</u>: The Layman's Bible Encyclopedia, 1964, Pg. 373, "The original Hebrew text of the Old Testament was written with out vowels, The name of God was represented by consonants JH WH. After the exile, no one except the temple priests pronounced this name; in it place was read or spoken the word adhonai (Lord).

<u>Metaphor</u>: the Random House Dictionary of the English Language, College Edition 1968, Pg. 840, 1. the application of a word or phrase to an object or concept it does not literally denote. In order to suggest comparison with another object or concept, as in "A mighty fortress is our God"

My metaphor was the statement saying His pure white fleece.

<u>Fleece</u>: The Random House Dictionary of the English Language, College Edition, 1968, Pg. 503, 1. "the coat of wool that covers a sheep or similar animal".

Christ was considered the "Lamb of God" In the Holman Home Bible, King James Version, Pg. 1087, St. John 1:29 "The next day John seeth Jesus coming unto him and saith, Behold the Lamb of God, which taketh away the sin of the world."

The Prince of Peace: The Holman Home Bible, King James Version, Pg. 729, Isaiah 9:6, "For unto us a child is born, unto us a son is given; and the government shall be upon his shoulder: and his name shall be called Wonderful, Counselor, The mighty God, The everlasting Father, The Prince of Peace".

King of Kings: The Holman Home Bible, King James Version, Pg. 1271, Revelation 17:14 "These shall make war with The Lamb, and the Lamb shall over come them: for He is Lord of lords and King of Kings: "and they that are with him are called, and chosen, and faithful".

Pg. 1223, 1st Timothy 6:15 "Which in His time he shall shew, who is the blessed and only Potentate," King of Kings, and Lord of Lords.

HOLY, HOLY. HOLY: The Holman Home Bible, King James Version, Pg. 727, Isaiah 6:3 "And one cried unto another, and said, Holy, Holy, Holy, is the Lord of host; the whole earth is full of his glory".

PG 1218, Revelation 4:8 "Each of the four living creatures had six wings and was covered with eyes all around, even under his wings, Day and night they never stop saying; HOLY, HOLY, HOLY is the Lord God Almighty, who was, and is and is to come"

Giving His Father the Glory: The Holman Home Bible, King James Vision, Pg. 1262, Revelation 4:11, Revelation 4:11, "You are worthy, our Lord and God, to receive Glory and honour and power, for you created all things, and by your will they were created."

The Holman Home Bible, King James Version, Pg. 1160, Romans 4:20 He staggered not at the promise of God through unbelief; but was strong in faith giving glory to God;"

Savior & Saviour: The Random House Dictionary of the English Language, College Edition, 1968, Pg. 1172, 1."A person who saves or rescues" 2."a title of God or Christ."

Your Lord God and Saviour: The Holman Home Bible, King James version, Pg. 1223. 2nd Timothy 1:10, But is now made manifest by the appearing of our Saviour Jesus Christ who hath abolished death, and hath brought life and immortality to light through the gospel:

Pg. 1210, Philippians 3:20, For "our conversation is in heaven; from whence also we look for the Saviour, the Lord Jesus Christ:"

We praise, praise the Lord God Jehovah

And thank Him over and over

For giving us life, through the blood of Jesus Christ

His pure white fleece, the Prince of Peace

The King of King's and Angel's sings

HOLY, HOLY, HOLY,

We give His Father the Glory

With much favor we present, your Lord God and Savior

Jesus Christ Your King

Ending:

Jesus Christ your King: The Holman Home Bible, King James Version, Pg. 1140, The ACTS 17: 6-7, 6. "And when they found them not, they drew Jason and certain brethren unto the rulers of the city, crying, These that have turned the world upside down are come hither also: 7. "Whom Jason hath received: and these all do contrary to the decrees of Caesar. Saying that there is another King, one Jesus."

Pg. 1273, Revelation 19:16 "And he hath on his vesture and on his thigh a name written, KING OF KINGS, AND LORD OF LORDS."

Jesus Christ your King

Jesus Christ your King

Acknowledgements:

This book and song was written to give Glory to God in the Highest. Through our Lord and Saviour Jesus Christ. Thank you God for loving us so much that you gave your only begotten Son to take our sin's from the world, and that through your grace we might live. Thank you so much from the bottom of my heart. In the name of Jesus Christ, I thank you.

This book and song was also written for the love of my children J. Clay and Paige Renee, my grandchildren, Michael, Ethan, Isabella, and Cecelia, and the children of the world that they might know God, through Jesus Christ.

Thank you Pastor Curt Duncan of the Laura Christian Church, Laura, Ohio, for all the time and effort it took in the music arrangement of this song.

I give thanks to Mike Sievers, for helping Curt Duncan with the CD and Mastering the CD on an Alesis Masterlink.

Thank you Blaine Heeter for transcribing the song into sheet music.

Thank you CD Solutions of Pleasant Hill, Ohio for all the work they put into making my CD a great piece of work and all the extra work they did on it. Thanks.

A thank you goes to Kathleen Kuhbander for proof reading my book and Query submission letter.

Thanks too, for the love and support of my family, my Mom, Betty, Sister Debbie and Brother Bob, and in Loving Memory of my Dad, Ira Roger Warman and Brother Roger Wayne Warman.

For the support of my friends through out my life. Those who are still here with me and those who have past. Carrie McCarroll, Lorinda Schlafman, Linda Willis and Dawn Carter and in memory of Barbara Dugus, and Freda Reaster. I miss you two.

A big thank you to my Husband Doug, for having the patience and tolerance and support that he gave me while recording and putting this song book together.

To hear the song and compose,
please visit this website:

JesusChristYourKing.com

and enjoy a free download.

www.ingramcontent.com/pod-product-compliance
Lightning Source LLC
LaVergne TN
LVHW072128060526
838201LV00071B/4993

9798330296309